# Max

Written by Jo Windsor
Illustrated by Martin Bailey

Max went to stay
with some friends.
He was sad.

He went to sleep on the mat.
He dreamed about Colin.
He dreamed about home.

Max sat under the tree.
He was sad.

He went to sleep on the mat.
He dreamed about Colin.
He dreamed about home.

Max sat by the gate.
He looked for Colin.
He did not want to stay.
He wanted to go home.

# Wednesday

He went to sleep on the mat.
He dreamed about Colin
and home.

Max played with the dogs.
He barked and barked.
It was fun.

He went to sleep on the mat.
He dreamed about the dogs.

Max played with the children.
He ran after the stick.
He barked and barked.
It was fun.

He went to sleep on the mat.
He dreamed about the children.

Max ran after the cat.
He ran and ran.
The cat ran and ran.

Max could not catch the cat!

He went to sleep on the mat.
He dreamed about the cat.
He wanted to catch that cat!

Max went home.

At home,
he went to sleep on the mat . . .

# A Diary

Dream Diary

Monday

Tuesday

Wednesday

Thursday

Friday

Saturday

Sunday

# Guide Notes

**Title: Max**

**Stage:** Early (2) – Yellow

**Genre:** Fiction

**Approach:** Guided Reading

**Processes:** Thinking Critically, Exploring Language, Processing Information

**Written and Visual Focus:** Diary, Symbol

**Word Count:** 184

## THINKING CRITICALLY
(sample questions)
- What do you think this story could be about?
- Why do you think Max is sad?
- How can you tell what time of day it is?
- What is the same about how Max feels in the day and in the night?
- How do you think Max feels at the end of the story?
- How do you feel when you have to stay away from home?
- How would you act if you were homesick?

## EXPLORING LANGUAGE

### Terminology
Title, cover, illustrations, author, illustrator

### Vocabulary
**Interest words:** dreamed, Monday, Tuesday, Wednesday, Thursday, Friday, Saturday, Sunday
**High-frequency words (reinforced):** went, to, he, was, some, by, the, under, home, did, no, want, go, after, could, on
**New words:** stay, friend, about
**Positional words:** under, by

### Print Conventions
Capital letter for sentence beginnings and names (**C**olin, **M**ax), full stops, exclamation marks, commas, ellipsis